IR

NATIVE AMERICANS IN THE WEST

Vic Kovacs

PowerKiDS press

Published in 2016 by **The Rosen Publishing Group, Inc.**
29 East 21st Street, New York, NY 10010

Developed and produced for Rosen by BlueAppleWorks Inc.

Art Director: T.J. Choleva
Managing Editor for BlueAppleWorks: Melissa McClellan
Designer: Joshua Avramson
Photo Research: Jane Reid
Editor: Marcia Abramson

Illustration & Photo Credits: Cover, p. 4 Charles Marion Russell/
Public Domain; title page Albert Bierstadt/Public Domain; cover,
title page, back cover (skull) Jim Parkin/Shutterstock; cover, title
page (wood) Dagmara_K/Shutterstock; back cover background
homydesign/Shutterstock;background siro46/Shutterstock; chapter
intro backgrounds rangizzz/Shutterstock; p. 9 Charles Bird King/Public
Domain; p. 10 François Bernard/Public Domain; p. 12, 26 Charles Marion
Russell/Public Domain; p. 16-17 Edgar Samuel Paxson/Public Domain;
p. 18 Henry F. Farny/Public Domain; p. 20 F. A. Rinehart/Public Domain;
page 20 background C. S. Fly/Public Domain; p. 23 Public Domain; p. 25
Carlyn Iverson; p. 28 Tyler McKay/Shutterstock

Cataloging-in-Publication-Data

Kovacs, Vic.
Native Americans in the west / by Vic Kovacs.
p. cm. — (The true history of the Wild West)
Includes index.
ISBN 978-1-4994-1173-7 (pbk.)
ISBN 978-1-4994-1203-1 (6 pack)
ISBN 978-1-4994-1195-9 (library binding)
1. Indians of North America — West (U.S.) — Juvenile literature.
2. Indians of North America — West (U.S.) — History — Juvenile
literature.3. Indians of North America — West (U.S.) — Social life
and customs — Juvenile literature. I. Title.
E77.4 K68 2016
970.004'97—d23

Manufactured in the United States of America

CPSIA Compliance Information: Batch #WS15PK
For Further Information contact: Rosen Publishing, New York, New York at 1-800-237-9932

CONTENTS

Many native cultures adapted quickly to horses, which Europeans brought to America.

Struggle for the Land

The first groups of people who would come to be known as Native Americans made their way to North America about 12,000 years ago. It's generally agreed that groups crossed over from **Eurasia** on the **Bering land bridge**, which connected Siberia to Alaska. In time, these first settlers spread all over the continent. As the population grew, unique tribes emerged. These tribes possessed their own languages, cultures, and ways of living. Many were **nomadic** hunter-gatherers, others were farmers who settled in one place and practiced **agriculture**. Some were experts in fishing, while some raided other tribes for crops.

These long-established ways of life began to change starting in the fifteenth century, with the arrival of European explorers and settlers. The first of these settlers came from Spain, and claimed many lands in the southern part of North America.

When settlers from other European countries such as France, England, and the Netherlands began to arrive on the east coast, they claimed lands there and even more as they moved west. European settlers routinely **displaced** Native Americans from lands they had been using for thousands of years. These European settlers also carried diseases that the Native Americans had no **immunities** to, such as smallpox. These diseases spread like wildfire, and it wasn't unusual for entire villages to be wiped out by them after their first encounter with Europeans. The demand for land increased after the American Revolution, when more and more settlers began moving west.

Estimates of the number of Native Americans living in what would become the United States vary hugely. Some experts place the number at around two million, while others say there were as many as 18 million. What is known is that by the year 1800, a mere two hundred years after the beginning of European colonization, the number was down to 600,000. On May 28, 1830, Congress passed the Indian Removal Act.

MYTH: Native Americans were few in numbers, and the land was "empty" for the most part.

TRUTH OR MYTH? This is a myth. Experts estimate that millions of people lived in modern-day America when the first European settlers arrived. This belief might stem from the fact that many Native American tribes did not have permanent settlements. Land that appeared empty one season might be a popular hunting ground the next. This was in keeping with the belief of many peoples that nobody could "own" land. People stayed in one place as long as it provided for their needs, and moved on when it didn't. The land would then have time to replenish itself when they were gone.

This allowed the U.S. president to negotiate land **treaties** with native peples. Native Americans who had lived east of the Mississippi for generations were pressured to leave their homes and move west of the great river. Though it was supposed to be a **voluntary** process, many Native Americans who didn't wish to leave their **ancestral** lands found themselves forced out to make way for white settlers.

Sequoyah, a Cherokee, brought reading and writing to his people in 1821. He created a system of symbols for Cherokee syllables.

The Plight of the Southeast Peoples

By the time of the Indian Removal Act, the Cherokee, Creek, Choctaw, Chickasaw, and Seminole peoples were known as the "Five Civilized **Tribes**." This name came from the fact that these tribes had adopted many of the customs of the white settlers. They lived in the southeast region of United States, mostly in farming villages. Though they were known to usually get along with settlers, they were often regarded as a nuisance. More and more people were moving south and west, and Native Americans there were occupying good, farmable land that settlers wanted for themselves to grow crops. This led to many clashes between whites and Native Americans. The Cherokee often had to deal with settlers stealing livestock or burning their homes in attempts to drive them off their land. The Cherokee repeatedly went to court to try to gain some measure of protection, but their attempts were unsuccessful.

This all culminated in 1830 with the passage of the Indian Removal Act. The act gave the government the power to give tribes unsettled land west of the Mississippi in exchange for lands they already possessed in existing states. This was supposed to be a voluntary process, and for some it was. The Choctaw signed a treaty in September 1830, and the majority moved west to what would become known as Indian Territory, which became the state of Oklahoma. Some Seminoles had moved to the Everglades in Florida.

The tribes that refused to leave quickly found that it wasn't a voluntary process as they had originally been told. A small group

The Choctaws had to build new villages in Oklahoma. They lived in cabin-like homes with cornfields around them.

The journey from their long-held ancestral homelands to the newly created Indian Territory was difficult and often deadly for Native Americans. About 16,000 Cherokees refused to leave their lands, and they were forced into **stockades** and then marched on foot for more than 1,200 miles (1,931 km). Along the way it's estimated between 4,000 and 5,000 died. The causes for these deaths were many. Diseases such as whooping cough, dysentery, and cholera were widespread. Often there wasn't enough food, so starvation was common. The journey was made on foot, and weather could be harsh, claiming many lives.

of Cherokee signed the removal treaty. However, this group was not made up of the accepted leaders of the Cherokee people, and the vast majority of Cherokee did not agree to the treaty. Despite this, the U.S. Congress ratified the final version in 1836, and demanded the Cherokee move west within two years. When most didn't, in 1838 the United States sent troops to force them out. These forced migrations collectively became known as the Trail of Tears.

Once they began riding horses, native hunters could get much closer to buffalo.

Changes on the Plains

The Great **Plains** stretch from North Dakota to Montana in the west, and all the way south to parts of Texas and New Mexico. Many native peoples called this area home, among them the Sioux, the Blackfoot, the Comanche, and the Lakota. The majority of Plains peoples became nomadic hunters, following buffalo from place to place without permanent villages. They used bows and arrows that were specially designed for buffalo hunting. The guns that were available at the time were too heavy and inaccurate, and took too long to reload to be practical. In time, as guns became lighter and more available, guns began to come into heavy use.

The buffalo was the cornerstone of the Plains Native Americans' way of life. They moved where the buffalo moved.

MYTH: All Native Americans were fierce enemies of U.S. Army soldiers and settlers.

TRUTH OR MYTH? This is a myth. Many Native Americans actively traded with settlers. Others served as guides, helping them make it through unfamiliar territory to their destinations. The fur industry was huge in the new world, and many of the most talented trappers were Native Americans. In the army, they often worked as scouts, and both the Confederacy and the Union had Native American soldiers during the Civil War. There were also many Native Americans who found success as cowboys, maybe the most famous American job of the nineteenth century.

Plains Native Americans were famous for being able to use every part of the animal once it had been killed. From its hide they would make clothing and shoes. Hides were also used to make teepees and tents that families lived in, which were easily broken down and packed up when it was time to move on. Buffalo hair was used to make rope, bones were fashioned into tools, and of course the meat was one of their primary sources of food.

Unfortunately, this reliance on the buffalo would prove to be their undoing. After a series of conflicts with white settlers, starting in the 1860s, both the U.S. Army and federal government encouraged the complete slaughter of the buffalo. There were a few reasons for this, such as creating more space for cattle to roam and helping to keep train tracks clear. The main goal, however, was to starve the Plains Native Americans off their land. In just three years, 1872 to 1875, about nine million buffalo were killed. By the 1880s, there were just a few hundred of the animals left. With their way of life in tatters, many Plains Native Americans reluctantly moved to **reservations**.

The Great Sioux War of 1876

In 1868, leaders for the Lakota people of the Great Sioux Nation signed the Fort Laramie Treaty with the United States. This treaty gave them the western half of South Dakota as the Great Sioux Reservation. Located on this land was an area known as the Black Hills, which was sacred to the Lakota. Other than government officials, nonnatives were forbidden from entering these lands.

Colonel Custer stands at center in this famous painting of the Battle of the Little Bighorn.

However, when gold was discovered there in 1874 it became nearly impossible to keep prospectors, miners, and settlers out. In 1875, the army officially stopped ejecting settlers from the Black Hills, and in December, all Native Americans in the region were told to move into a reservation set up for them elsewhere. Native leaders didn't want to leave their land, though, and refused the order. As the deadline to leave came and went, the battles that would be known as the Great Sioux War of 1876 began.

The most famous of these clashes between the Sioux and Cheyenne warriors and the U.S. Army is probably the Battle of the Little Bighorn.

The army had sent three groups of soldiers to fight the Native American warriors. One group included Colonel George Armstrong Custer, a well-known veteran of the Civil War. Coming upon a group of Lakota, Cheyenne, and Arapaho warriors along the Little Bighorn River in Montana, Custer decided to attack, instead of waiting for reinforcements. Custer didn't realize how many native warriors were present. Most estimates point to around 1,800 compared to around 600 men under Custer. Custer and the 200 men in his battalion were killed in the battle. This was the largest win for the Sioux in the war, as well as the worst defeat for the army. It was still just a single battle, however, and in the end, the United States emerged victorious.

Sitting Bull

A Hunkpapa Lakota holy man and chief, Sitting Bull was a well-known and respected warrior by the time the Great Sioux War of 1876 began. One of the few remaining chiefs to refuse all government assistance, he refused to relocate to reservations. Shortly before the Battle of the Little Bighorn, during a ceremony called the Sun Dance, he had a vision of his people defeating U.S. soldiers. This inspired them, and probably helped it come true the day of that fateful fight. Afterwards, to escape retaliation from the U.S. Army, Sitting Bull and his people moved north to Canada in 1877. Four years later, due to being unable to hunt enough buffalo there to survive, he returned to the United States and surrendered. In 1890, his arrest was ordered, as it was feared he was about to flee the reservation. As he was led from his home by force, he resisted, and one of his supporters

Towards the end of the Wild West era, performances presenting an idealized version of the era became popular. Known as Wild West Shows, these exhibitions included reenactments of historical battles, sharpshooting events, and horse races. The most famous of all of these was called Buffalo Bill's Wild West Show. Run by Buffalo Bill Cody, it started in 1883. One of his main attractions was Annie Oakley, an incredible sharpshooter. Oakley met Sitting Bull while she was touring, and the two became great friends. It was through this friendship that Sitting Bull came to join Buffalo Bill's Wild West Show. Sitting Bull's part in the show was pretty simple. During the opening parade, he would ride out on a horse, and then circle the arena in a single lap. After only four months, Sitting Bull returned to the reservation. Upon hearing of his killing, his friend Annie Oakley remarked that if he were a white man, "someone would have hung for his murder."

shot at the arresting officers. They, in turn, shot Sitting Bull twice, once in the head and once in the chest. A gunfight broke out that left eight native police officers dead, as well as seven Lakota loyal to Sitting Bull.

Geronimo became a symbol of bravery. After seeing a movie about the Apache warrior, a U.S. paratrooper began the World War II tradition of shouting "Geronimo" when making a jump.

Pushing Towards the West Coast

As the United States expanded its borders westward, it continued to come into conflict with Native Americans. The Apache people, located in the southwestern United States, and the Nez Perce in the northwest were next to be pushed out of their lands.

Apaches waged continual war first against Mexico and then the U.S. government for many years until famed Apache leader Geronimo and his last followers surrendered. The Apache were then forcibly settled on reservations.

Apaches and Geronimo

A fierce Apache warrior, Geronimo fought for decades against the advancement of Mexicans, and later U.S. settlers, into his people's lands. The fight wasn't just about territory, though. One day, while Geronimo was away from his camp, it was attacked by Mexican soldiers. Upon returning, he found that his mother, wife, and three small children had been killed.

MYTH: The U.S. government neglected Native Americans on reservations.

TRUTH OR MYTH? Yes and no. The federal government created many laws to protect Native Americans on reservations. The government also set laws providing native peoples with necessities such as food and clothing. Unfortunately, many of the officials in charge of the reservations were **corrupt** and would sell these goods to white settlers instead of distributing them. So even though laws required Native Americans to be treated well, individual **corruption** often ruined the government's intentions.

Geronimo became a source of terror for Mexicans and then for U.S. settlers as the United States took control of areas where his people traditionally lived. Geronimo raided Mexican and U.S. settlements, and took on the status of living legend in the press. His final surrender came in 1886. He would live the rest of his life as a prisoner of war of the U.S. government. On his deathbed, it's said he told his nephew, "I should never have surrendered. I should have fought until I was the last man alive." Geronimo died in 1909.

The Nez Perce

In the northwest, things weren't much better for Native Americans. The Nez Perce, located in Idaho, Washington, and Oregon, were one of the largest peoples in that area. They lived in permanent villages in the winter, and traveled to the same locations every year to hunt during the other seasons. In 1855, they signed a treaty guaranteeing them exclusive use of large parts of their ancestral lands. Unfortunately, gold was discovered on their land in 1860. In a situation very similar to what was faced by the Sioux on the Plains, their land was invaded by prospectors, miners, and other white settlers.

The Nez Perce lived in family groups. Women had key roles and could speak at council meetings.

Despite their treaties, the U.S. government refused to do anything about the squatters. In 1863, certain leaders of the Nez Perce were pressured into signing away most of their land. Other leaders refused, and this divide created two groups: The "treaty" Nez Perce and the "non-treaty" Nez Perce. The treaty Nez Perce moved onto a new reservation in Idaho, while the non-treaty Nez Perce stayed on the land they never agreed to give away.

Chief Joseph and the Nez Perce War

After his father's death in 1871, Chief Joseph became leader of one of the "non-treaty" bands. Although they were harassed by whites who had shown up looking for gold, Chief Joseph enforced nonviolence from his people, preferring to make **concessions** to them. This unsteady peace lasted until 1877, when his people were ordered to relocate to the reservation. Even after they were given an impossible deadline to do so, Chief Joseph continued to advocate for peace, knowing that they could not win against the might of the U.S. Army. After several young men from the tribe killed

Chief Joseph spoke out for his people until his death in 1904 on a reservation.

four white settlers, the choice was out of his hands. Knowing that the army would retaliate, Joseph, along with other chiefs, moved their people north, hoping to find refuge in Canada. In reality, the Nez Perce War was their retreat, during which they constantly outfought and outmaneuvered the army chasing them. It turned out that Chief Joseph, the longtime pacifist, was something of a military genius. He even earned the nickname "The Red Napoleon," after a famous French general. In the end, his people managed to flee for over 1,000 miles (1,600 km). However, after a five-day battle in freezing weather, Joseph was forced to surrender. He and his people were just 40 miles (64 km) away from the Canadian border.

The move to reservations ended the nomadic way of life for many native peoples.

The New Beginnings

By the turn of the twentieth century, the Native American way of life was in danger of disappearing. The once plentiful buffalo that many tribes had hunted for their survival were nearly extinct. The lands that they had called home for many generations had been taken and settled by whites. Instead of roaming over vast swaths of land, they were now mostly confined to reservations.

Life on the reservation was often tough. Native Americans were urged to become more like white settlers. They were encouraged to abandon the cultures and customs they had practiced for hundreds of years. Regardless of how they had survived before, they were now told to become farmers. Even tribes that had practiced agriculture previously often found the land unsuitable for growing crops. As a result, food was often scarce. They were also often punished for wearing traditional clothing or speaking anything but English language.

Schools were established to teach Native American children, but they were often kept home. Parents feared that their children would grow up ignorant of their traditional ways if they were taught only to be "American." Officials in charge of the reservations were also occasionally corrupt, furthering the native peoples' distrust of whites.

Preserving Traditions

In 1924, with the passage of the Indian Citizenship Act, all Native Americans became citizens of the United States. Today, they occupy every level of American society. Many have chosen to move to large urban areas. Los Angeles and New York City both

Today, many Native peoples share their heritage at celebrations called powwows.

Sarah Winnemucca

Sarah Winnemucca was born around 1844 to the Paiute people in Nevada. With a natural gift for languages, she was a talented interpreter, scout for the military, activist, and speaker, and later in her life, an educator. Her biggest claim to fame is as a writer. In 1883, after years of speaking engagements and lectures where she described the plight of her people, and spoke out about the corruption of many reservation officials, Winnemucca turned her lectures into a book. Titled *Life Among the Piutes: Their Wrongs and Claims*, it was also the first book in English published by a Native American woman.

are home to large populations of Native Americans. Many others remain on reservations, where peoples' councils constantly work to make life better for everyone. Many groups have opened colleges, where Native American students can learn about their culture as well as earn degrees and train for jobs. Many Native Americans have become successful artists, using their art as a way to spread their cultures. Many museums and galleries have entire sections devoted to Native American art. Today's Native Americans are proud of their heritage, and will do whatever it takes to keep it thriving.

Glossary

agriculture Using the land to grow plants and animals, for eating as well as other uses.

ancestral Belonging to a person's past relatives, or ancestors.

Bering land bridge A strip of land that connected North America and Asia during the Ice Age but is now underwater.

concessions Something done or agreed to usually grudgingly in order to reach an agreement or improve a situation.

corrupt Guilty of dishonest practices, such as bribery.

corruption Dishonest behavior and dealings by those in power.

displaced Put out of its traditional or usual place.

Eurasia The name of the continuous landmass that, separately, is known as Europe and Asia.

immunities Physical qualities that keep a person from getting a disease.

nomadic A word to describe a person who continuously travels to new areas instead of settling and staying in one place.

plains An area of land characterized by its general flatness.

reservation An area of land set aside for use by Native Americans.

stockade A fenced area, often in a fort, where prisoners may be held.

treaty An agreement between two groups, often formalized in a document.

tribe A group of people of the same culture, often connected by family ties.

voluntary Not forced, done by free will.

For More Information

Further Reading

Cornelissen, Cornelia. *Soft Rain: A Story of the Cherokee Trail of Tears.*
New York, NY: Random House, 2009.

Gibson, Karen Bush. *Native American History for Kids: With 21 Activities.*
Chicago, IL: Chicago Review Press, 2010.

Mcgovern, Ann. *Native American Heroes.*
New York, NY: Scholastic, 2014.

Spinner, Stephanie. *Who Was Sitting Bull?*
New York, NY: Penguin Group, 2014.

Websites

Due to the changing nature of Internet links, PowerKids Press has developed an online list of websites related to the subject of this book. This site is updated regularly. Please use this link to access the list:
www.powerkidslinks.com/thoww/native

Index